B2B SALES, SIMPLIFIED!

MASTER B2B SALES — NO-GURU, NO- INFLUENCER WAY

If you can handle three

Venti lattes, you can handle this book — and master B2B sales for real.

SCOPE OF THIS BOOK

WHO IS THIS BOOK REALLY FOR?

LET'S KEEP IT SIMPLE.

This isn't a book filled with "10X closing secrets," "no call sales hacks," or the kind of chest-thumping motivation you find in guru driven reels. You won't learn how to hypnotize a prospect in 30 seconds.

Why? Because that stuff doesn't work in real-world B2B.

What you'll find here is a **step-by-step guide to selling your B2B solutions** — the kind of selling that requires patience, structure, discipline and above all emotional intelligence.

This book is ideal for you if:

- You're **starting your career in B2B sales** and don't want to waste years figuring it out the hard way.

- You're **coming from another profession** (like marketing, engineering, or customer service) and want to transition into solution selling with clarity.

- You're **already in B2B sales**, but feel like your approach is too random — and want a cleaner, more repeatable structure.

- Or maybe... you're just tired of the fluff, and ready to learn how real deals are built and closed.

If that sounds like you — you're in the right place.

These steps aren't complicated. They're not revolutionary. But they work — and when applied with consistency, they'll make you a **trusted, effective, and fulfilled** sales professional.

Now let's get to it.

FAQ

Before you dive in, let's clear a few more things up.

What do you mean by "B2B Solution Selling"?
B2B Solution Selling is about selling **complex B2B offerings** — like software, IT services, or customized systems — where the buyer isn't just picking a product, but solving a real business problem. This book draws from my own experience selling such solutions, and everything here is built for that world.

Is this book useful for selling consumer products (B2C)?
Not really. Some universal sales principles apply, sure — but this book is focused on **B2B solution sales**, where more direct communications, relationships, customizations, and longer sales cycles are the norm.

What level of experience is this book written for?
If you're just starting out in B2B sales — perfect.
If you're a few years in and want more structure — even better.
If you're a senior sales pro, some parts might feel basic, but it can still give you a clean framework to revisit or coach others with.

Will this book help me improve my sales techniques?
Yes — but not by throwing one-liners or hacks at you.
It gives you a **systematic approach** to selling: how to qualify,

discover, demo, and handle proposals, close, and more— so your sales game becomes smarter and more repeatable.

Does the book focus on any specific industry?

My background is in software and ICT, so that's the natural lens. But the principles of solution selling apply across most B2B sectors — from SaaS to consulting, logistics to manufacturing.

Do I need any prior knowledge to use this book?

A basic understanding of how B2B sales works is helpful — but not required.

If you're coachable, curious, and serious about improving, this book will meet you where you are.

ABOUT ME

I've spent nearly two decades in B2B sales, working across software, IT, and telecom — leading multimillion-dollar deals and managing accounts worth over $100 million in revenue. I've worked with global brands like Ericsson, Huawei, ZTE and VyOS Networks, and have sold complex solutions across multiple countries in the globe.

But the numbers don't define me.

I'm not a "natural closer" or a born salesman. I started as a software engineer. My strength has always been showing up, taking risks, being courageous — yet with discipline, consistency, and a drive to keep improving. I don't chase shiny tactics or magic scripts. I focus on what works, and I keep learning.

When I was working full-time in a demanding IT role, I studied for my MBA in the evenings — sometimes rushing straight from the office to class with nothing but a chocolate bar in my pocket. I didn't even finish my marketing course before I was promoted to marketing and sales manager at a multinational company. That's the kind of learning curve I've lived through.

In 2021, I migrated from my home country to Australia — no local network, no insider connections. I was told I wouldn't land a sales job because "sales is market dependent." But I knew better. B2B sales, at its core, is like engineering — it's about solving problems and communicating value. Within three months of landing, I landed my first business development role through pure application and interview — no referrals, no shortcuts. Just preparation and clarity.

This book isn't built on theory. It's built on real experience — wins, failures, and everything in between. If you want a practical roadmap to succeed in B2B solution selling, minus the fluff and guru talk, I wrote this for you.

Feel free to connect with me in LinkedIn and check my credentials: https://www.linkedin.com/in/imrul/

BEYOND THE BOOK
Help is Available

Real-World Help. Anytime.

This book isn't just a standalone guide. It is part of a growing knowledge ecosystem I've built to support your B2B sales journey — grounded in real-world experience, not theory.

- At the center is SalesMind.online, a learning hub packed with free, practical resources:
- Articles on real sales scenarios
- Templates and tools you can use immediately
- Personal stories from the field
- And regular updates on how B2B selling is evolving

You'll also meet Bucky — your AI Sales Consultant. Bucky is trained not just on this book, but on my years of experience and proven B2B strategies you won't find from a search engine. You can use it to:

- Ask follow-up questions on topics from the book
- Practice prospecting messages, discovery conversations, or objection handling
- Get quick help refining a cold email or prepping for a meeting
- Challenge your thinking when you're stuck

Whether you're starting out, changing industries, or just tired of bad sales advice — SalesMind.online offers a practical, honest, and modern approach to B2B selling.

Note: SalesMind.online is a solo project — built, written, and managed entirely by me. It's still evolving, so you might notice rough edges. But stay tuned — I'm constantly improving it, one post and one feature at a time.

ONE LAST NOTE

BEFORE YOU START - READ ME

Before you dive in, let's set the record straight.

I've spent nearly 2 decades in B2B sales — across multiple countries, thousands of customer conversations, and deals worth tens of millions. And here's what I've learned:

There's no "sell-like-crazy" magic formula.

No "Straight Line / Curve Line / Parallel Line Method."

No secret magic script (sorry!).

No abracadabra (unfortunately!).

If there were, the gurus selling them wouldn't need to flood your feed 24/7/365 (and 366 days in a leap year) trying to convince you to buy their coaching program. Actually selling a coaching program is much easier than sealing an actual sales deal.

Here's the truth:

Sales is built on five basic pillars — discipline, integrity, ownership, consistency, and communication.

That's it. That's the game.

A little psychology helps. Creativity doesn't hurt.

But unless you're selling iPhones — the kind of product

people camp out overnight for — there's no hack that replaces real effort and skill.

If you're ready to build those skills the right way —

Let's get started.

THREE TERMS TO REMEMBER

Customer - Leads - Prospects

Let's get to very basic at the beginning.

Customer:

A customer is someone who has already made a purchase from your business. They've bought your product or service and established a relationship with your company.

Prospect:

A prospect is someone who has shown interest in your product or service and has the potential to become a customer. They've likely interacted with your business in some way—such as signing up for a newsletter, attending a demo, or downloading a resource—but they haven't made a purchase yet.

Lead:

A lead is identified as someone who could be interested in your product or service. While they might not know much about your business yet, they fit the profile of a person who could benefit from what you offer.

- **Warm Lead:** A warm lead has already shown some level of engagement, such as visiting your website multiple times, interacting with your content, or expressing interest in your services. They are more likely to convert into a customer than cold leads.

- **Cold Lead:** A cold lead is someone who has been identified as a potential prospect but hasn't shown much interest or engagement with your business yet. They may be unfamiliar with your brand or not yet aware of how your product can benefit them.

Difference:

- **Leads** are individuals who may be interested but need further qualification.

- **Prospects** are leads who have shown more genuine interest and engagement, and are closer to becoming customers.

- **Customers** are people who have already made a purchase and have established a relationship with your business.

Think of it as a funnel: leads are at the top, prospects are in the middle, and customers are at the bottom.

STAGES OF B2B SALES

1. Understanding the scope of the solution

2. Understanding your target customer

3. Lead generation

4. Prospecting

5. Introductory Communication

6. Discovery

7. Demo or Budget Qualification

8. Follow up discussion

9. Proposal Submission

10. Negotiation

11. Closure – Win or Learn

STEP#1
UNDERSTANDING
THE SCOPE OF
THE SOLUTION

Which problem can your solution solve?

"If you can't explain it simply, you don't understand it well enough." — Albert Einstein

Successful B2B solution selling starts with a clear understanding of the business problem your solution addresses. Simply put, as a sales representative, you need to know which problems your solution will solve for the customer.

Remember, the word "solution" implies solving a problem or addressing a need. If you can't articulate what problem your solution solves, it will be difficult to create value for your customers.

If your solution doesn't save time, reduce costs, or improve the customer experience for your customers, no matter how sophisticated it is, it will not resonate with your prospect.

Creating a Fitting Value Proposition

When you have a deep understanding of your solution's value, you'll be able to:

- Tailor your pitch and messaging to address customer pain points.

- Respond to customer questions with confidence and clarity.

- Differentiate your product from competitors.

Key Point:

As a salesperson, it's crucial to understand your solution's value proposition well enough to communicate it effectively. If the discussion requires more technical depth, involve a pre-sales technical expert. Your role is to guide the customer in recognizing your solution's value.

Example:

If you're selling software that extracts data from invoices and converts it into an editable Excel/CSV format, you don't need to know how the coding works. Instead, understand that this feature eliminates the time-consuming, manual data entry process, making accounts payable more efficient for your prospects.

Problem Solved:

- Reduces manual data entry time

- Increases operational efficiency and saving cost.

Pro tip:

You may have heard this from many so-called sales gurus: "I sold this and that without even knowing much about it — my pitch was just that good." I'll say this — No, not in B2B.

You might get lucky once, but in real B2B sales, you're dealing with well-informed buyers. These are educated decision-makers who've usually done their homework before speaking with you. If you think you can simply charm them with charisma, without offering something truly relevant or feasible — expect to be ghosted after one meeting. Effortlessly.

Take the time to deeply understand your solution and its benefits. That's what earns trust, opens real conversations, and keeps you in the game.

STEP#2
UNDERSTANDING
YOUR TARGET
CUSTOMER

Who has the problems that your solution may solve?

"Stop selling. Start helping." — Zig Ziglar

Once you understand the value your solution provides or the problem it solves, the next step is to identify the business organizations or individuals experiencing those specific problems or seeking that value—and, most importantly, those willing to invest in solving the issue or achieving greater efficiency.

If you're a new business owner, launching a new solution, or entering a new market, this step is crucial for establishing an effective sales function.

5 Key Actions to Identify Your Target Customer:

1. Define your target customer by creating detailed buyer personas.

2. Identify their needs and pain points that align with what your solution addresses.

3. Determine the value your solution delivers to solve these pain points.

4. Understand your target customers' organizations,

including their purchasing patterns and decision-making hierarchies.

5. Analyze the competition to differentiate your offerings and find unique selling points.

Note: It's recommended to document all of these actions to create a clear strategy. Keep this document dynamic and update it periodically as you gain more market insights.

Example:

Let's say you're selling a CRM solution designed to streamline customer interactions and provide data-driven insights. Your target customers could be small-to-medium-sized businesses struggling with fragmented customer data and inefficient follow-up processes.

- *Customer Need:* They need a way to consolidate customer information and automate follow-ups to improve their sales efficiency.

- *Solution Value:* Your CRM provides a single platform for storing customer data and tracking interactions, automates follow-up emails, and offers sales forecasting reports. This helps reduce manual data entry, eliminates missed opportunities, and provides visibility into the sales pipeline.

Problem Solved:

- Disorganized customer data.

- Inconsistent follow-ups.

- Lack of insight into sales performance.

By addressing these pain points, your CRM solution helps businesses save time, increase sales efficiency, and make data-backed decisions.

REFLECTION TIME

***

Take a pause and get your pen and paper or notepad.

Reflect on Step 1 & Step 2 above and ask yourself these Qs:

Am I fully aware of the capabilities of my solution?

If yes - Great Job!

If no - Put a task in your everyday to-do list to build competence on solution's values that you are selling.

Note down the 5 key actions to identify your customer. Ask

yourself, do I have clear information on these 5 points? If no - Take action based on your answers – target gradual improvements.

***

STEP#3 LEAD GENERATION

Who may like to discuss what your solution can do for them?

"Action is the foundational key to all success." — *Pablo Picasso*

By now, you're comfortable with the solution you're selling and have a decent understanding of your target customers. Now comes the challenging (and to some extent exciting) part — generating leads from that target group.

In large organizations, entire teams are often dedicated solely to lead generation. They warm up prospects and pass them on to the sales team. However, in many cases, especially in growing companies or specialized markets, you'll be expected to handle this part yourself. That's why building some core lead generation skills is not just useful — it's essential.

Some Proven Ideas for Lead Generation:

- **Referrals:** Happy customers are your best advocates. Encourage them to refer your solution to others. Word-of-mouth can be a powerful, low-cost lead generation engine.

- **Inbound Marketing:** Create content that pulls customers toward you — blog posts, whitepapers, case studies. Optimize your website to capture interest and turn visitors into prospects.

- **Outbound Marketing:** Be proactive. Cold emails, cold calls, and direct messaging (especially on LinkedIn) can put you in front of decision-makers before they even realize they need you.

- **Partnerships:** Collaborate with other businesses or vendors in your industry. Strategic partnerships can open doors to new networks and customer bases.

- **Networking:** Build your network consistently — both online and offline through genuine empathetic conversations - it's not the networking event, it's building a real network.

- **Social Media:** LinkedIn is your best friend for B2B lead generation. Engage, connect, share valuable content, and stay visible.

- **Paid Social Media Ad:** Platforms like LinkedIn, Facebook, and especially YouTube are now prime spaces for B2B lead generation. Think about how often you see ads from software or SaaS companies while watching a business or productivity video on YouTube — those aren't random. They're targeted lead generation ads designed to capture decision-makers in the right mindset. If done right, paid ads can drive high-quality traffic to your site and generate warm leads at scale. Just make sure your ad copy speaks to a real problem and leads to a clear, valuable next step.

- **AI Tools:** Stay sharp. New AI tools can automate prospecting, help you find contact information, and even personalize your outreach at scale. Being tech-savvy gives you an edge.

- **Networking Events:** Webinars, trade shows, and conferences are goldmines for networking. Use LinkedIn before, during, and after events to connect with potential leads.

- **Your Own Website:** Your own website can be a powerful lead generation tool — if built right. Use SEO to attract relevant search traffic, add smart forms to capture warm leads, and integrate with a modern CRM to track who is visiting and what they're interested in.

You'll often see the term *"hunter mentality"* in sales job descriptions — and for good reason. Lead generation truly is a hunt. You need to seek out opportunities actively, not wait for them to come to you.

One critical piece of preparation: craft a strong, targeted opening message. Your first outreach should focus squarely on the prospect's pain points and how you can help solve them — **not** on your company's branding or how great your product is. Remember, at the start, people care less about who you are and more about how you can help them.

Brand recognition and company reputation will support you later — after you have established credibility and earned their trust.

Pro Tip: You must have a company LinkedIn page. Once you (or whoever manages it) post something about your solution or brand, make sure every employee shares it from their own profile. It's organic, it's free, and it massively increases your reach.

REFLECTION TIME

✳✳✳

Reflect on your lead generation activities and ask yourself these questions:

Am I clear about who my target customers are and what problems they face?

Do I have a basic lead generation strategy in place (referrals, inbound, outbound, partnerships, events, networking)?

Am I consistently working on improving my outreach message to focus on the prospect's problems first?

Am I aware of and using the latest tools (like AI and LinkedIn) to assist my lead generation efforts?

If yes — Great Job, you're building the foundation of a true sales hunter.

If not — Set a clear daily or weekly task to sharpen your lead generation skills.

***

NOW TAKE A BREATHE AND LAUGH A LITTLE

The Networking Events That Led to Absolutely Nothing

Among all the lead generation strategies, one that's never really worked for me is... **networking events or Trade Shows** - I don't even mention it for the right reason.

Maybe it's just me. Maybe I'm not the "working the room" type. But I've found most networking events follow a reliable structure:

- People arrive.
- People grab a drink or Collect freebies from trade show booths
- People attack the free finger food like it's their first meal in days.
- Everyone chats, nods, and says things like *"Let's connect!"*
- Then... silence.

To give you a **real life** example, I once attended a networking event (among many) hosted by a well-known enterprise software company and their user community. I was invited because I was offering a solution that integrated directly with their platform — something designed to enhance the experience for their existing users.

Perfect fit, right? - Right audience, right context, and a clear value-add. I thought I hit the jackpot.

I handed out business cards. I had decent conversations and explained a little on how the solution can help ... People even said, *"That's interesting, send me something tomorrow!"*

So I did. The next day, I followed up like a professional. Sent personalized emails, offered short discovery calls, kept it friendly and tight.

Guess how many replies I got? - **Zero.** Not even a "not now" or a "who is this?" Just pure digital silence.

Let's just say the finger food had a higher conversion rate than my follow-up emails.

STEP#4 PROSPECTING

Let's connect with the people you can help with your solution

"The secret of getting ahead is getting started." — Mark Twain

Prospecting is a huge topic — entire sales careers are built around doing it well (or avoiding it). But for now, let's focus on the fundamentals to help you get moving with clarity.

What Is Prospecting, Really?

Prospecting is the process of identifying potential customers and generating leads to build a pipeline of qualified prospects. It goes beyond just "finding names" — it's about planning **how** to reach out, and **why** someone should even care.

You can think of prospecting as the bridge between lead generation and communication. If you've already identified your target customer profile and gathered some good leads, prospecting is how you organize, qualify, and approach them.

Core Prospecting Steps: Here's how to approach it with structure and intent:

a.   **Research potential customers:** Use tools like LinkedIn, company websites, and industry directories to find organizations that match your ideal customer profile. Identify decision-makers by role — and always check for recent news, changes, or activities that can give you context.

b.   **Use your network:** Before you reach out cold, ask yourself - ***Do I know anyone at this company?*** Friends, ex-colleagues, someone from a past project — they're gold. Grab a coffee, have a casual chat, and learn how the company operates. What's their internal hierarchy? How do they make decisions? This kind of "insider info" is often the fastest route to meaningful engagement — and it's shockingly underused. I've leaned on this consistently in my career.

c.   **Choose the best channels:** Think about how your prospects prefer to communicate. For tech buyers and decision-makers, email and LinkedIn usually work best. In some cases, calling or even warm intros might be the way to go. Your choice of channel should match **who they are** and **what stage of awareness they're in**.

d.   **Craft Sharp, Relevant Messaging:** Your message should feel like it was written **for them** — not just copied and pasted. Focus on their pain points, and how your solution addresses them. Keep it short, conversational, and useful. If you've got relevant case studies or results, bring them in — but only if they're tight and aligned.

e.   **Set a follow-up plan:** Don't be the salesperson who gives up after one message. Follow-up is where most deals are built — **but** don't become spammy. Create a follow-up plan with a clear rhythm (e.g., 2-3 touchpoints over 2 weeks), and vary the content. Try a different angle, offer value, or share a resource. But remember - *follow up like a machine - don't give up easily!*

Example from work - Combination of Lead Generation & Prospecting:

In one of my recent roles, I spent about an hour a few times a week prospecting on LinkedIn. One of our solutions was a great fit for IT MSPs, so I filtered contacts by relevant roles. If someone accepted my connection request, I'd start a short, honest conversation around their current tech challenges and where we might help. If it clicked, I'd suggest a short remote call — no pressure.

Was it fast? Not really.
But it worked — and the key was **consistency and patience**.

Thoughts

Prospecting isn't about magic words or hacks. It's about showing up, every week, with a plan and a purpose. You won't win every conversation — but you'll learn from each one.

Start small. Stay consistent. And keep the radar on.

REFLECTION TIME

✳✳✳

Take a pause and get your pen and paper or digital notepad.

Reflect on steps Lead Generation & Prospecting above and ask yourself these Qs:

Do I have a rich pipeline full of leads and prospects?

If YES - Fantastic Job.

IF NO - dig down deeper with the following Qs:

Do I have a clear lead generation and prospecting strategy in place?

Am I dedicating a fixed amount of time every day/week to perform activities related to lead generation and prospecting?

Find answers to these Qs - note down your strategy and plan as a part of the answers of these Qs.

You will be surprised with the results you will get within 30-60 days of disciplined and consistent work.

✱✱✱

Continue Prospecting - Communication with Prospects

"The most important thing in communication is hearing what isn't said." — Peter Drucker

This is where the real game of sales begins.

You've done the groundwork — you know your solution, you understand your target customer, and you've generated leads. Now it's time to turn conversations into opportunities.

Sales communication is the engine that moves everything forward. There are many ways to reach a prospect today — from social media and live chat to video messages and beyond. But in this step, we'll focus on the **mainstream, battle-tested channels** that still drive most results in B2B sales:

- **Cold calls**
- **Cold emails**
- **LinkedIn**
- **Thoughtful follow-ups**.

Mastering these core channels is your key to opening doors and starting real sales conversations.

COLD CALL

In modern B2B selling, cold calling is not a one-size-fits-all strategy. It may work brilliantly in some cases — and fall flat in others. The effectiveness of a cold call largely depends on the **type and structure of the organization** you're targeting.

For example, **in small, owner-driven businesses**, cold calls can still be very effective. You're often speaking directly with the decision-maker, and if your message is clear and relevant, you can generate quick interest or even secure a meeting on the spot.

But for **larger, more complex organizations**, things aren't that simple. These companies operate through multiple layers — procurement teams, technical evaluators, and department heads. In such cases, cold calling without understanding who holds influence, how the buying process works, or what stage of the decision-making cycle they're in is often a waste of time. Randomly dialing into these organizations without context is like shooting in the dark.

That's why cold calling **isn't about dialing fast and closing hard** — it's about **precision, preparation, and purpose**.

The goal of your cold call is not to sell your solution over the phone. In B2B solution selling, your real target is simple: **book the next meeting** — the discovery call where you can understand the client's challenges in detail.

You don't need a flashy pitch — just a thoughtful, well-prepared approach:

- Do your homework. Personalize based on their role,

company, or news.

- Focus on pain points, not product features. Lead with relevance.

- Ask simple, relevant, smart questions to build trust.

- Keep your tone confident, clear, and respectful.

- Ask for an appointment, not a decision. Propose a next step.

- Don't push. Invite a conversation.

- If possible, get their email and immediately follow up with a brief summary of the discussion. This shows professionalism and keeps the conversation alive.

Done right, cold calling is still a powerful tool in your outreach toolkit — but only when used with intelligence and context.

COLD EMAIL

Like cold calls, **cold emails** can be a powerful B2B outreach tool — when done right. But in today's overloaded inboxes, getting noticed takes more than just a catchy subject line.

And just like cold calling, the effectiveness of cold emailing depends on **who you're targeting**.

- If you're reaching out to **a small company** or **a founder-led business**, a well-written, personalized cold email might reach the decision-maker directly — and get a quick response.

- But for **larger organizations**, your email could easily get lost unless you're laser-targeted, relevant, and credible. You might be emailing someone in procurement, IT, or operations — each with a different perspective and level of influence. That's why knowing **who to email** and **what matters to them** is just as important as how you write the email itself.

In solution selling, the goal of a cold email isn't to close a deal in one go, it's just not possible — it's to **spark interest and start a conversation**.

A solid cold email should be short, simple, and focused on the **prospect's world**, not your product.

Here are key principles to follow:

- **Personalize** your message. Use their name, mention something relevant about their business, role, or industry.

- **Start with their problem.** Show them you understand a

challenge they're likely facing — don't lead with a product pitch.

- **Offer a short value-focused hook.** One or two lines explaining how you help solve that problem — ideally with a simple, specific benefit.

- **Include a clear, low-pressure CTA.** For example: *Would it make sense to explore this in a quick 15-minute call next week?* Or even, something like *would you like to get more details?* Sometimes I simply do - *"Let me know your thoughts ..."* [Yes with 3 dots ending that line].

- **Make it easy to skim.** Use short paragraphs and avoid jargon. No one reads a wall of text from a stranger.

- **Follow up.** One email is rarely enough. Most replies come after 2–6 (or more) polite and relevant follow-ups.

And one honest truth — even the best cold emails won't always work. That's okay. What matters is consistency, testing, and continuous improvement.

If your message is relevant and respectful, and you're targeting the right people, cold emailing is still one of the most scalable ways to start meaningful sales conversations — especially in modern B2B.

LINKEDIN

When it comes to B2B sales, **LinkedIn is no longer optional — it's essential**.

Whether you're targeting small business owners or senior decision-makers in large enterprises, LinkedIn is often the most direct and credible channel for starting a conversation. But just like cold calls and cold emails, how effective it is depends on **how you use it.**

Let's assume you've already built a prospect list — either from inbound leads or outbound research. LinkedIn can help you do three things:

1. **Find the right person** within the organization.

2. **Understand their background, role, and interests.**

3. **Connect and start a conversation in a non-intrusive way.**

Before you send a connection request, do your homework. **Are they the right person to talk to?** Can you find a **mutual connection** or recent post to reference in your message?

You don't need a fancy message. In fact, a simple, respectful approach works best.

Here's an example that has consistently worked for me:

"Hi [Name],
It would be a pleasure to connect with you.
Regards,
[Your Name]"

If you're reaching out to someone very senior (like a Chairman or C-level executive), a small touch of added respect can make a difference:

"It would be an honor to connect with you."

Once you're connected, take the time to engage thoughtfully:

- **Look at their posts**, company updates, or recent activities.

- **Like, comment, or mention** something relevant when you follow up.

- Don't rush into a pitch — build familiarity and context first.

LinkedIn InMail - is it effective?
Despite all the hype, I've personally never had success with it — and I've tested it at scale. Even with polished messages and psychological techniques, response rates were near zero. That doesn't mean you shouldn't try, but don't rely on it as your main strategy.

Last but not the least, focus on **building a presence**:

- Keep your profile professional and clear about what you do.

- Share helpful content or insights occasionally.

- Use LinkedIn as a place to connect with people — not just to sell, but to **start relevant conversations**.

In today's B2B landscape, your LinkedIn activity is part of your digital first impression. Treat it like your online business card and conversation starter — not your sales pitch.

What works – a real life example of my LinkedIn prospecting?

TUESDAY

Shah Imrul Huq [in] (He/Him) • 10:55 AM

Hi ▮▮▮,

Good morning. We have been connected for a while and I am trying to see if I can add any value ...

I have recently found visits from ▮▮▮▮▮ in VyOS website. I would love to know if I can connect your team with our solution architect if there is any query ...

Please let me know - I am happy to help. I also work from Brisbane, if you feel a face to face meeting is a good idea, please let me know, happy to meet up for a coffee ...

BR/Shah.

▮▮▮▮▮ (He/Him) • 10:56 AM

👍

Thanks Shah I'll chat with the team and be in touch

Shah Imrul Huq [in] (He/Him) • 10:56 AM

Sounds, great, is it okay to share your work email ID?

▮▮▮▮▮ (He/Him) • 10:58 AM

▮▮▮@▮▮▮com.au

Shah Imrul Huq [in] (He/Him) • 10:58 AM

Thank you. I'll drop the latest datasheet to your emai and will be happy to hearing from you ... Cheers/Shal

▮▮▮▮▮ (He/Him) • 10:59 AM

Thanks Shah

👍 1   😊

Pro Tip: It's not necessary to post about your grocery shopping on LinkedIn and force a leadership or sales lesson out of it. People praising the post in the comments might actually be laughing behind the scenes. Recruiters may see it as an attempt to appear wise—when it clearly doesn't come across that way. Instead, focus on sharing how your solution solves real problems in the industry and benefits the companies using it. That's what truly demonstrates your skill, passion, and wisdom.

REFLECTION TIME

✳✳✳

Reflect on how you're showing up in this crucial phase:

Am I confident and prepared before making a cold call?

Are my messages focused on the prospect's pain points, not just my product?

Do I personalize my emails and LinkedIn messages based on real insights?

Am I using tools (like AI, CRM System etc.) to save time and stay consistent?

Do I have a clear call to action in every outreach?

If you answered yes to most — great job, you're building real sales momentum.

If not — pick just one area to improve this week, and commit to small, consistent action.

✲✲

NOW TAKE A BREATHE AND LAUGH A LITTLE

The Scripted Cold Call That Went Nowhere

Let me share one of the most unintentionally funny cold calls I've received — the kind that shows exactly how blind scripting can crash a sale in seconds (B2C example though).

It started with a call from someone representing an electricity provider. The rep jumped straight into a pitch about rising government electricity rates and how their company could help me save money. The only problem? They never asked whether I even had the authority to change providers — which I didn't. I live in a rented home, so I can't just switch electricity providers on a whim.

I told them politely, "I'm not the one who decides that here."

Instead of acknowledging or adjusting, they pivoted — not based on relevance, but clearly just moving to the next item in their script. "What about your internet?" they asked.

Now I was curious to see how deep into this "sales coaching special" they were. So I said, "Sure, what's the offer?" They gave me a number that was maybe slightly cheaper than my current plan — not nearly enough to make me even consider switching.

So I said the honest (and universal) thing: "I'll need some time to think about it."

At this point, I could hear the sales script kicking in like clockwork. The rep immediately asked, "How long do you need?" I replied, "Maybe two weeks." I was just playing along at this point — I knew where this was heading.

Sure enough, they went in with one of the most recycled sales lines of all time:
"What will change in two weeks that's stopping you from deciding now?"

At that moment, I had to laugh. Not sarcastically — genuinely. I told the rep, "Look, not all objections are made-up. Some are just real. No script can fix that."

And then... *click.* The call ended. No goodbye. No closing statement. Just awkward silence and a disconnect.

STEP#5 DISCOVERY PHASE

My Prospecting Was Good - Time to Impact Positively

"Understanding is a two-way street."
— Eleanor Roosevelt

The discovery meeting is one of the most critical stages in solution selling. This is where you, as the sales professional, gather detailed information to understand your prospect's needs, challenges, and pain points. The goal of this meeting is to uncover as much relevant information as possible so you can tailor your proposal to fit the specific needs of the client.

1. **Preparation:** Before the discovery meeting, research your prospect thoroughly. Understand their industry, business model, and any recent news or challenges they may be facing. Review the information gathered during the introductory communication phase, and be ready to ask targeted, insightful questions.

2. **Conducting the Meeting:** During the discovery meeting, the focus should be on active listening. Ask open-ended questions that allow the prospect to elaborate on their challenges. Your objective is to understand their problem, not to sell them anything at this stage. Avoid diving into a sales pitch too early.

3. **Uncovering Needs:** Dig deep to uncover both the explicit needs (the ones they are aware of) and the implicit needs (the ones they may not be aware of

but which your solution can address). Understanding these needs will allow you to create a compelling value proposition later in the process.

4. *Asking the Right Questions* - Asking the right questions is key to uncovering valuable insights during the discovery phase. Your questions should encourage the prospect to open up about their pain points, challenges, and goals. By doing so, you can dig deeper into their situation and reveal hidden needs that they might not even be fully aware of. These insights will help you tailor your solution to address their specific challenges, ultimately making your proposal much stronger.

5. **Soft Skills - Empathy and Active Listening:** Empathy and active listening are crucial soft skills in the discovery phase. Demonstrating empathy shows that you genuinely care about the prospect's challenges, while active listening helps you capture important details and nuances in their responses. Together, these skills build trust and rapport, which are essential for moving the sale forward.

6. **Building Trust:** This meeting is not just about gathering information but also about building trust. Show empathy, understanding, and professionalism. Make the prospect feel that you genuinely care about solving their problem, not just making a sale.

To make things easier to understand I made a framework (not claiming it's anything revolutionary) – using this you can perhaps easily remember the steps of a discover meeting:

Discovery Framework: A.S.K. M.O.R.E.

A – Ask Open Questions
Get them talking freely.
S – Show Empathy

Listen like you care — because you do.

K – Know the Stakes
What happens if they don't fix the issue?

M – Map the Buying Process
Who's involved? What's the timeline?

O – Outline the Success Vision
What does "done right" look like to them?

R – Reveal Gaps
Subtly highlight where your solution could help.

E – Establish the Next Step
Always close with a clear follow-up.

What Not to Do

One of the most common mistakes I've seen is sales professionals opening discovery meetings with a long, scripted company profile — "We do this, we've done that," often for 10+ minutes. It sounds impressive to the speaker, but for the buyer, it's usually boring and irrelevant — and it kills momentum early. No matter how proud you are of your brand, resist this urge.

Instead, focus entirely on the client. If the meeting goes well, you can offer to share a brief overview of your company at the end — and do it in under five minutes, ideally supported by a relevant case study or reference that connects to their situation.

Pro Tip: The reason this section is called the "Discovery Phase" and not just "Discovery Meeting" is simple — it often takes more than one meeting to uncover everything you need. Follow-up discussions, clarifications, and alignment points are common, especially in complex B2B sales.

What matters most is this: keep your prospect informed at every step. Be clear about why additional conversations may be needed, and what each one aims to achieve. Transparency builds trust — and shows that you're guiding the process with purpose.

REFLECTION TIME

***

Take a moment to review your approach to discovery meetings.

Are you asking the right questions?

Are you truly listening to your prospects?

Are you using empathy to connect with your prospects on a deeper level?

Write down three ways you can improve your discovery meetings moving forward.

***

STEP#6 DEMO OR BUDGET QUALIFICATION

Choosing the right next move after discovery.

"He will win who knows when to fight and when not to fight." — Sun Tzu, The Art of War

After the discovery meeting, it's time to move the opportunity forward — but what you do next depends on what you've learned.

Some prospects are highly interested but want to see proof. Others are interested, but their buying ability is still unclear.

That's why this stage can go in two directions:

- If the **prospect clearly understands their problem** and needs to see how your solution works → it's time for a **demo**.

- If there's **uncertainty about purchasing authority, timing, or budget** → focus first on **budget qualification**.

Trying to push a demo before a prospect is ready can waste time. And asking about the budget too early — before trust and value are built — can shut down the deal.

Pro Tip: Deeper understanding on human behavior and organizational structure and power base of prospects will help you a lot here.

Here are some guidelines to help decide which path to take:

When to do a Demo:

- The prospect is already familiar with the issue and seems eager to solve it.

- They've asked for a walkthrough or want to see how your solution works.

- They've invited others from their team to join a discussion.

- You're in a competitive sales situation and need to show differentiation.

- You're selling a product or platform that's visual or feature-driven (common in IT/software).

When to do Budget Qualification First:

- The prospect's interest feels casual or exploratory.

- They haven't clarified who the decision-makers are.

- You suspect there may be a mismatch in budget expectations.

- You're unsure if they're ready to invest or just gathering information

- If prospects and you are not aligned on the commercial/pricing model.

This is a Judgment Call — and It Matters

This is one of those moments in sales where no script can help you — only your judgment can. Whether you go for a demo or move into budget qualification depends entirely on what you've uncovered, how well you've read the situation, and how tuned in you are to the buyer's mindset. There's no universal rule — just signals, context, and experience. And this decision often shapes the entire outcome of the deal. A well-timed move builds momentum. A rushed or misjudged one can quietly derail everything. Trust your gut — but make sure it's an informed gut.

RUNNING A GREAT DEMO (ESPECIALLY FOR TECH/IT SOLUTIONS) – A FEW HELPFUL TIPS

In technical sales, your demo is **not** a product tour — it's a solution story. It should directly connect what the prospect said in discovery to what you show on screen.

Here's how to do it right:

1. Personalize It

Open by saying: "Based on our last conversation, I've focused this demo on the area's most relevant to [their challenge]."
This sets the tone that it's not generic — and they'll pay more attention.

2. Solve, Don't Show

Every feature you show should be tied to a benefit or pain point discussed. If they talked about slow reporting, show how your dashboard solves that — don't show every dashboard function.

3. Simplify the Language

If you're working with non-technical buyers, strip out the jargon.

Translate features into business impact: "This automation saves your team 6–8 hours a week."

4. Tell a Story

Use real-world scenarios. "Imagine you're onboarding a new client..." or "Let's walk through what happens when your team logs in on a Monday."

5. Confirm Engagement

Ask questions during the demo, like:

- *"Is this how your current process looks?"*

- *"Would this approach make things easier for your team?"*

6. End with a Recap

Highlight the key pain points addressed and confirm next steps — either another stakeholder meeting, proposal, or budget discussion.

Remember: A great demo doesn't impress — it connects.
The goal is not to wow with features, but to make them say, "That's exactly what we need.

Again, for memorization, I develop a Demo Framework – Use it to structure you demo:

The S.A.L.E.S. UP Framework

A Practical Demo Flow to Present Solutions with Clarity and Confidence

S – Set the Scene

Start with a 30-second context. Remind them of the core problem discussed in discovery. Align expectations: "Here's what we'll show, and why it matters."

A – Anchor the Pain

Briefly recap the prospect's current challenge or inefficiency. Don't over-explain — just connect their problem to what's coming.

L – Link the Solution

Transition into your demo by saying: "Let me show you how this solves what you're facing." Make it about *them*, not your product.

E – Explain with Relevance

Show the key features **that matter most to them** — nothing flashy. Stick to what addresses their pain, not what's "cool."

S – Show the Value

Narrate the impact. "Here's how this saves time," or "This is where most clients see ROI." If possible, use brief data or results from similar customers.

U – Use a Story

Tell a quick real-life example: "A customer like you had X problem — after using this, they got Y." Make it relatable and short.

P – Prompt Next Steps

Wrap up by asking a soft but clear question:
"What's your initial impression?" or
"Should we explore how this fits your workflow further?"

Pro Tip: Don't Demo Unnecessary Fancy Features

Avoid the temptation to show off every fancy capability your solution offers — especially if it's not directly tied to the client's problem. Even if a feature looks impressive, if it's irrelevant to their need, it can distract the discussion, raise unnecessary questions, or even create pricing objections. Sometimes the client will ask about a shiny feature just out of curiosity — but later push back to get in included in the pricing for free (real life experience). Keep your demo tight, focused, and problem-driven. Less noise, more relevance.

RUNNING A SMART BUDGET QUALIFICATION CONVERSATION

Budget discussions can feel sensitive — but they don't have to be uncomfortable. If you've built trust during discovery, this part of the conversation becomes a natural next step. The goal isn't to corner the prospect — it's to make sure you're both aligned before investing more time and resources.

Here's how to handle it with confidence and care:

1. Position the Discussion Naturally

Don't launch into numbers out of the blue. Ease into the conversation by framing it as a mutual step forward:
"To make sure this is a good fit for both sides, would it be okay if we also explored the budget and decision process?"
This shows professionalism and sets the tone for a collaborative discussion.

2. Ask Open, Framing Questions

Rather than bluntly asking, "What's your budget?" guide the conversation with questions that give context and insight:

- *"Have you already set aside a budget range for solving this issue?"*

- *"How does your team typically approach investments like this?"*

- *"Are you the final decision-maker, or are there other stakeholders involved in the budget approval process?"*

These questions help you understand not just the number, but the process behind it.

3. Be Direct, But Respectful

If the prospect is vague or hesitant, it's okay to gently push for clarity:

"We work with a wide range of clients and offer different approaches depending on budget. Having even a rough idea helps us tailor the right recommendation for you."

This keeps the conversation value-focused without sounding aggressive.

4. Link Cost to Value

When price inevitably comes up, avoid defending the number. Instead, connect it back to the outcomes you've already discussed:

"Yes, the investment is $X, but it typically saves teams 20–30 hours a month in manual work. That's why most of our clients recover their investment in the first 3 to 6 months."

When the conversation is anchored in value, pricing becomes less of a barrier.

5. Know When to Walk Away

Not every lead is worth pursuing — and that's okay. If you learn there's no real budget, no urgency, and no decision-maker involved, it's a clear sign to qualify out.

Avoid the trap of chasing unqualified prospects just because they were "interested." Time is your most valuable resource in sales. Use it wisely.

Focus your energy on opportunities that show real potential — not polite dead ends.

Pro Tip: I recommend avoiding the word **"budget"** entirely in your budget qualification conversations. In many cases, the word itself can trigger discomfort or resistance — especially early in the sales process. As a sales professional, your first goal should always be to **disarm your prospect and reduce friction in the conversation**.

Instead, consider using words that sound more strategic or growth-oriented. For example, use **"investment"** when speaking with mature enterprises, and **"funding"** when dealing with startups or innovation-focused teams. Here's how you can reframe:

- **Old:** "Have you already set aside a budget range for solving this issue?"
  New: "Have you already secured funding for this project?" or "Have you developed an investment plan for this initiative?"
- **Still good:** "How does your team typically approach investments like this?"
- **Instead of:** "Are you the final decision-maker, or are there other stakeholders involved in the budget approval process?"
  Try: "How does the investment or funding process typically work for a project like this in your organization? What kind of decision chain is involved? I'd love to understand so I can align my communication better."

These alternatives soften the conversation and put you in a more collaborative light.

Adapt each statement based on your prospect's personality and business context — language is a powerful tool when used with emotional intelligence.

REFLECTION TIME

***

Take a pause and reflect on how you're handling this crucial decision point in your sales process.

Ask yourself:

Am I rushing into demos just because the prospect seems interested?

Do I take time to qualify whether the customer has the authority, urgency, and budget to move forward?

Are my demos personalized and tied directly to the pain points uncovered in discovery?

Do I approach budget conversations with confidence, not hesitation?

Am I willing to walk away from unqualified opportunities to focus on better ones?

If you're answering *yes* — you're thinking like a trusted advisor, not just a seller. If not — this is your chance to slow down and sharpen your judgment before diving into proposals or presentations.

***

STEP#7 PROPOSAL SUBMISSION

Putting it all together with clarity and confidence.

"Well begun is half done." — **Aristotle**

Proposal submission is a **big milestone** in the sales process — but it's not as straightforward as it sounds.

There's no one-size-fits-all format for proposals. In fact, depending on your industry, pricing model, or the type of solution you're offering (e.g. fixed price, subscription, outcome-based, or implementation-heavy), the structure and content of your proposal can vary greatly.

Some clients may ask for a formal RFP-compliant proposal, others expect a simple business case slide deck. The key is to **match your proposal to the buying process and preferences of your client**.

What I've shared in this section is not an exhaustive framework — but a set of **core principles** that can dramatically improve the impact of any proposal, regardless of format.

Think of these as your **"non-negotiables"** for effective proposal writing:

1. Make It Tailored, Not Generic

A generic proposal is easy to spot — and easy to ignore.
Start strong by clearly connecting your solution to the pain points and goals uncovered in the discovery phase. Reference their challenges by name. Use their language. The more personal it

feels, the more seriously it will be taken.

If you've ever received a pitch deck that looked like it was blasted to 50 companies with the name swapped out — you know how that feels. Don't be that seller.

2. Be Clear and Concise

Proposals aren't the place to show off jargon or write a novel. Your message should be clean, structured, and outcome-focused.
A busy stakeholder should be able to skim your proposal and still understand:

- What the problem is
- What you're offering
- How it solves the problem
- What success looks like

Stick to plain, professional language. Add visuals or tables where needed — but keep them purposeful, not decorative.

3. Focus on Outcomes, Not Features

Make sure your proposal clearly states the results the client will achieve — not just what the solution includes.
Instead of:
"Our platform includes automated data sync and real-time dashboards."
Say:
"Your team will save 12+ hours per week by eliminating manual reporting, while gaining real-time insights for faster decision-making."

Outcomes are what decision-makers buy — features are just how you get there.

4. Include a Strong Executive Summary (Start or End)

It's a great idea to include a one-page executive summary

at the beginning of your proposal. This is especially important if multiple stakeholders will review it — some of whom may not have been part of earlier conversations.

In one clear page, summarize:

- The prospect's key challenges
- Your recommended solution
- Expected business outcomes
- High-level costs and next steps

Busy decision-makers will thank you — and more importantly, they'll get your message even if they never read the full proposal.

5. Follow Their Format (if it's a must), but Add Your Own Layer

If the client has provided a prescribed format (such as an RFP template or structured form), follow it precisely — but don't stop there.

Always include a supplementary document that reflects *your understanding* of their situation. You can title it something like: *"Solution Justification and Value Summary."*

In this supporting doc, you can:

- Reframe their needs in your own words
- Reinforce the value your solution brings
- Clarify why this proposal is structured the way it is

This small step can be powerful. It gives you a voice beyond the form — and helps you stand out in formal buying processes.

6. Outline the Next Step

One of the most common mistakes in proposals? **No clear call to action.**

Don't assume the buyer knows what to do next. End with a simple, confident direction:

- *"We recommend a 30-minute review call to finalize scope and timelines."*
- *"If you're happy to move forward, we'll prepare the agreement for signature."*

Make the path forward easy and friction-free.

Pro Tip: It's strongly recommended to present and explain your proposal in a face-to-face meeting — especially if it's complex and contains multiple components that need clarification. This meeting also gives you valuable insight into how the prospect feels about the pricing, terms, and overall structure of the proposal.

REFLECTION TIME

Time to assess how strong your proposals really are.

Ask yourself:

Am I including a clear, compelling executive summary at the top of each proposal?

Do I follow the client's format *and* provide my own supporting value summary?

Are my proposals easy to skim, focused on outcomes, and tailored to the client's unique needs?

Do I guide the buyer with a clear and simple next step?

If yes — you're giving yourself a strong

chance to win every proposal you submit.

If not — now is the perfect time to revise your proposal process. One smart change here can make a big difference in your close rate.

STEP#8 NEGOTIATION

The best negotiations are won before they begin.

"The supreme art of war is to subdue the enemy without fighting." — Sun Tzu, The Art of War

Let me say this upfront — a lot of sales gurus won't like what I'm about to say.

But I'm not a guru. I'm a salesman. And I've learned most of what I know about negotiation the hard way — by losing deals I thought I had in the bag, by giving discounts I shouldn't have, and by walking away from conversations that went nowhere.

That's why I believe this:

Negotiation isn't where the deal is won — it's where the groundwork pays off.

If you've done your job well in the discovery, demo, and budget phases, negotiation should feel like a formality — not a fight.

Sun Tzu said, *"Victorious warriors win first and then go to war, while defeated warriors go to war first and then seek to win."*
In sales, that means winning the negotiation starts **long before** you sit at the table.

When a buyer asks for a deep discount or pushes hard on terms, it's often a signal of one of two things:

- They **haven't clearly understood the value** of your solution

- Or they're **not actually serious about buying**

- They have settled with your competition already

In any way, it points to a gap in earlier stages — not a failure in negotiation skills.

This is especially true in **RFP or tender-driven deals**. If your solution's key strengths and differentiators weren't included in the specs or evaluation criteria — you're likely already behind. The negotiation won't save the deal. If you're not shaping the deal early, you're reacting too late.

That Said... Strong Negotiation Skills Still Matter

Even when you've done everything right, you'll still need to close the gap between what the buyer wants and what you can offer. Strong, simple negotiation skills will help you close confidently — without giving away unnecessary value.

Here are practical skills every solution seller should master:

1. Know Your Walk-Away Point

Before entering any negotiation, define your bottom line:

- Minimum price
- Scope limits
- Contract flexibility

If things fall below that line, you're better off walking away than closing a painful deal.

2. Always Bring It Back to Value

If a client says, *"Can you drop the price?"*, your default response should be:

> *"Let's revisit what this solution will help you achieve."*

Tie every pricing conversation back to cost sav ings, efficiency, risk reduction, or revenue gain.

3. Trade, Don't Give

Never offer a discount without asking for something in return — a longer commitment, quicker payment terms, case study permission, or larger volume.
This reframes the conversation from *"Can you lower the price?"* to *"What can we both adjust to?"*

4. Stay Calm, Stay Professional

The more emotional you get, the more power you lose.

Keep the conversation objective and solutions-focused. If you feel rushed, slow down. If the client tries to apply pressure, hold your ground — especially if you've demonstrated strong value.

5. Clarify Scope Before Discounting

Often the client is trying to fit a fixed budget.
Instead of lowering the price, consider adjusting the scope. A slightly smaller solution today can be expanded tomorrow — without underpricing yourself now.

6. A Little Fear Factor Works — If It's Real

When appropriate, help the client consider what might happen if they don't act — **without exaggeration**.

- Will operational costs continue to rise?

- Will revenue opportunities be missed?

- Could customer satisfaction or retention be impacted?

If possible, **quantify that risk in simple financial terms**:

"Delaying this implementation by 6 months could mean $40,000 in manual processing costs that automation would have already eliminated."

But remember — your buyer also knows their business well. Stay respectful and grounded. Fear works best when it's **realistic**, not theatrical.

REFLECTION TIME

✳✳✳

Take a step back and reflect on how you approach negotiation — not just at the table, but throughout your sales process.

Ask yourself:

Am I setting myself up for a smooth negotiation by handling discovery, demo, and budget alignment properly?
Do I know and respect my walk-away point — or do I cave under pressure?
Am I defending my price with outcomes, not just features?
Do I make strategic trades, or just give discounts to win deals?
Am I helping the client see the real cost of inaction — clearly, and without exaggeration?

If you answered *yes* to most — you're likely negotiating from a position of strength.
If not — go back upstream. Strengthen your discovery. Sharpen your value message. The better your early game, the easier the closer.

***

NOW TAKE A BREATHE AND LAUGH A LITTLE

The Never-Ending Negotiation (That Wasn't a Negotiation at All)

Here's a classic one — and I won't even go into all the details because honestly, it still stings a little.

It started like many promising deals do: the client seemed interested, asked for a proposal, and even created a bit of *"urgency"* to get it by the end of the week. So I prioritized it, spent time building the right scope, pricing structure, and justification deck — all customized.

They responded quickly — to ask for a discount.

Then another revision. Then more trimming of the scope… and yet another "final price check."

Every time, they hinted they were *"almost ready to move forward."* They even looped in someone from procurement. I thought we were getting close.

Then came the punchline: *"If you can go 30% lower, we're in."*

At that point, I'd already spent over 30 hours across meetings, custom revisions, and internal alignment. And after all that? Nothing. No response. Not even a "thanks."

It wasn't a negotiation. It was a drawn-out price fishing expedition dressed up as a deal.

Visual Debrief:

- Time invested: 30+ hours
- Revenue generated: $0.00
- Number of follow-ups sent: Way too many
- Emotional damage: Let's not talk about it

Lesson: If you're doing all the work, all the chasing, and all the discounting — and they're just "thinking about it" — that's not a prospect. That's a time sink.

Sometimes the best negotiation move is to walk early — not crawl out exhausted.

FINAL STEP: DEAL CLOSURE

The Moment of Truth!

"You win some, you learn some." — John Maxwell

This is where it all leads — the close.

After all the calls, meetings, demos, and negotiations, the deal either comes together… or it doesn't.

But here's the truth: whether the deal closes or collapses, your work isn't over. In both scenarios, there's value to extract, lessons to carry forward, and relationships to manage — because today's "no" can turn into tomorrows "yes," and today's "yes" still requires careful follow-through.

The next two sections explore both sides of the outcome — because in B2B sales, success and failure are both part of the same game.

DEAL CLOSURE - SUCCESS

"In every success story, you will find someone who made a courageous decision."

— Peter F. Drucker

The sale is done, but your work isn't.

Closing a deal is a big moment — the result of everything you've done right: identifying the problem, presenting the right solution, building trust, and guiding the buyer through each phase with confidence.

But deal closure isn't just about contracts and celebrations. It's the start of a customer relationship, and how you handle this transition will often define the future of that relationship.

Celebrate, But Stay Professional

It is okay to feel proud — closing a deal in B2B solution selling takes real skill. Celebrate internally with your team, but with the client, stay professional. Thank them sincerely and reinforce your commitment to delivering value.

Ensure a Smooth Handover

Immediately coordinate with your delivery, onboarding, or implementation team. A smooth transition from sales to service is critical — it builds trust and sets the tone for long-term success. Brief your internal team well so the client doesn't have to repeat themselves.

Request Feedback

After the deal is signed, ask the client:

"What worked well during the sales process? What could we improve?"
This not only helps you grow — it shows maturity and long-term thinking.

Look Ahead — Upsell, Cross-Sell, and Stay Relevant

A closed deal opens new doors. As you maintain contact with the client, keep listening for future needs. Don't pitch too early — but when the time is right, recommend upgrades or complementary solutions based on evolving challenges.

Stay Connected and Visible

Even without immediate sales potential, stay in touch. Share relevant updates, invite them to events, or just check in. Staying top of mind protects your relationship from competitors and reminds them that you're invested in their long-term success.

Ask for Referrals, Testimonials, and Build a Case Study

Once the solution is implemented and value has been delivered, ask for a testimonial or referral — and make it a habit.
Even better, create a short customer success story or case study. This builds social proof and gives you powerful real-world examples for future prospects. Referrals and testimonials aren't just nice-to-haves — they're a must.

Pro Tip: Real-life lesson — never, ever celebrate too early. Even if you receive a verbal confirmation or a positive email from your prospect saying everything looks good and the decision is likely in your favor — don't let your guard down. It can break your heart.

Wait until the official purchase order or signed contract is in your hands. And even then... there's one more step. I'll keep that as a *secret* for now — you'll find out later in the book. Keep reading.

DEAL CLOSURE - FAILURE

"Failure is simply the opportunity to begin again, this time more intelligently."

— Henry Ford

When you don't win — make sure you still learn.

Not every deal will go your way. That's the reality of B2B sales — no matter how well you prepare or perform.

Sometimes, you'll lose a deal even after months of hard work. The reasons can range from price, timing, internal politics, procurement constraints, or even just bad luck. It stings. But **what matters most is what you do next.**

Don't Take It Personally

This is hard — but essential. A lost deal doesn't define your worth as a sales professional. Rejection happens to everyone in sales. Take a breath, and approach the situation with maturity.

Seek the Real Reason — Without Ego

Ask for honest feedback. Even if you only get 50% of the truth, it's better than staying in the dark. You can say: "I completely respect your decision — but if you're open to sharing, I'd really appreciate any feedback that could help me improve."

Sometimes the loss will come down to things outside your control. Other times, you'll learn something that sharpens your process.

Debrief and Learn from the Mistake

Don't just move on to the next lead. Do a quick internal **debrief session** with yourself or your team.
Ask:

- Where did we lose momentum?
- Was the proposal aligned with the buyer's actual priorities?
- Were there early red flags we ignored?
- Did we truly establish value?

Writing down these insights — even briefly — turns a painful loss into practical growth.

A failed deal without a lesson learned is a missed opportunity twice over.

Revisit When the Time is Right

Just because you lost the deal doesn't mean the door is fully closed. If the relationship was respectful, consider checking in after a few months. Business needs evolve, budgets shift, and sometimes competitors fall short.

Stay polite, stay visible — and when the timing is right, you will get another shot.

REFLECTION TIME

✳✳✳

Every win and loss has something to teach you — if you take the time to reflect.

Ask yourself:

What did I do well in my last few wins? How can I repeat that consistently?
Am I turning happy customers into success stories, referrals, or testimonials?
After a lost deal, am I seeking honest feedback and doing a proper debrief?
Do I have a habit of following up on lost opportunities after a few months?
Do I treat every deal closure — win or lose — as a moment to improve and build stronger relationships?
If you're taking the time to review, learn, and grow — you're already ahead of most.

SHAH IMRUL

***

SALES ISN'T ALWAYS LINEAR BUT YOUR DISCIPLINE CAN BE

The chapters in this book have laid out a structured, step-by-step approach to help you build the mindset, skills, and habits of a high-performing B2B sales professional. But let's be real — **the real world doesn't always follow a clean sequence.**

You may find yourself doing **multiple demos** before anyone brings up the budget.

Sometimes, the sales cycle may start with a pricing discussion before you even get to ask discovery questions.

Other times, you might be pulled into the process **after** a proposal has already been requested.

In large organizations, sales stages can be influenced by procurement, multiple decision-makers, and unpredictable timelines.

That's okay.

What matters is that **you've trained yourself to understand the full sales journey** — and you know what's missing, even when the situation isn't linear. That's what separates a professional from someone who's just reacting.

The more you grow in skill, patience, and awareness of the sales cycle, the better you'll be at adapting — without skipping steps that matter. And the better you understand **where you are in the journey**, the more confident and effective you'll be in guiding your buyer forward.

That's why having a clear internal map of sales stages — from prospecting to discovery, to demo, to proposal, and beyond — gives you a huge edge.

Structure won't guarantee success — but it gives you the foundation to win even in chaos.

SALES CULTURE

Creating a productive atmosphere for sales people

"Culture eats strategy for breakfast." — Peter Drucker

If you're a business owner or leading an organization, this part is especially for you.

Before you even hire your first salesperson, you must wear the invisible hat of "Head of Sales." Not in job title — but in mindset. Successful businesses don't just have sales teams; they have a culture that fuels and respects sales. That culture starts at the top.

A strong sales culture means creating an internal atmosphere where selling is supported, not silently blocked. It means you — as the owner — are actively working to raise brand awareness, increase visibility in the right markets, and make it easier for your team to build trust with customers. You don't just build a product or service; you build momentum behind it.

Internally, sales success doesn't end with a signed deal. If customer service fumbles after the sale, or project delivery falls short, that deal may actually do more harm than good. Sales is a team sport. HR, finance, legal, operations — every function plays a role in creating an experience that helps salespeople win and keeps clients coming back.

I've seen egos in departments destroy great opportunities. When internal teams act like gatekeepers instead of enablers — when they see themselves as "the boss" instead of part of the same mission — salespeople become demotivated, and deals stall. It's not always loud. Sometimes, it's just subtle delays, cold responses, or unnecessary friction. But the effect is real.

And here's the other side of the coin: I've also seen business owners completely step away from sales — delegating it entirely to their team while they focus only on processes and internal operations. Yes, those things matter. But when the owner is absent from the sales front, it weakens leadership. Your sales team doesn't just need tools. They need energy, clarity, and alignment. And that starts with you.

Build a sales culture where everyone understands that nothing happens until something is sold. Make sales everyone's business — and success will follow.

TENDER | RFP | RFQ

A few words about it

Over the years, I've participated in numerous tenders, RFQs, and RFPs — especially while working for large multinational companies. And here's the truth: while tenders may look like opportunities on paper, they're often massive time and resource sinks in reality.

Large enterprises can afford to participate. They have dedicated teams to prepare documents, chase clarifications, handle compliance, and absorb the opportunity cost if they don't win. But if you're working in a mid-sized or growing company, you need to ask a simple question before jumping in:

Can we afford the time, cost, and distraction — especially if we're not already shaping the spec?

In my experience, unless you were involved **before** the RFP dropped — during the "pre-tender" phase — and unless your solution is reflected in the specs or you have a strong relationship with decision-makers, submitting a proposal often ends up as a polite formality. You're there to make up the numbers.

This isn't to say you should never participate. Every situation is different. But be strategic. Don't assume every tender is worth chasing. Winning business through open RFPs requires preparation, positioning, and timing — not just a great proposal.

Use your judgment. Respect your time. And never confuse activity with progress.

Pro Tip:

Before committing to a tender, take a moment to reflect on your data.

Look at your typical **prospecting-to-close timeline**. Ask yourself:
If we didn't participate in this tender, how many new qualified

leads could we pursue — and how many deals might we actually close?

That simple comparison can help you make a more rational, resource-smart decision.

THE MINDSET THAT SEPARATES THE BEST

"You have power over your mind — not outside events. Realize this, and you will find strength." — *Marcus Aurelius*

Without addressing the mindset, no sales guide is complete.

Tactics, scripts, tools — they matter. But behind every top-performing sales professional is a set of core mental habits that power everything they do. Skills get you in the game, but **mindset keeps you in long enough to win**.

Sales is not always linear, easy, or fair. That's why you need mental strength, emotional awareness, and daily discipline — especially in high-stakes B2B selling. Below are the **key mindset traits** that define high-performing, consistently successful salespeople.

1. Relentless Resilience – Embrace Rejection

Top sales professionals don't fear rejection — they expect it. They treat every "no" as a step closer to "yes," and they use rejection as fuel, not failure. Each tough call sharpens their pitch.

2. Extreme Ownership – Take Responsibility for Results

No blaming the product. No blaming the client. High performers take full ownership. If they lose a deal, they learn. If they win, they prepare to deliver. Accountability breeds improvement.

3. Customer-Centric Thinking – Sell to Solve, Not to Close

The best salespeople don't pitch — they listen. They frame every conversation around solving real business problems. That's why they build trust fast and close with ease.

4. Unshakable Confidence – Believe in the Solution and Yourself

Confidence isn't arrogance — it's clarity. When you truly believe in your solution, it shows. Buyers feel it. Confidence gives your pitch weight, and your presence credibility.

5. Growth Mindset – Stay Curious and Keep Learning

The best never stop learning. Books, feedback, podcasts, or mentorship — they invest in themselves. They know what worked last quarter might not work today, and they adapt accordingly.

6. Daily Discipline – Win Through Consistent Action

Big wins come from small actions. Top sales pros don't just work hard when they're motivated — they show up every day with a plan. Prospect, follow up, repeat.

7. Emotional Intelligence – Read the Room

High EQ helps you sense hesitation, adjust your tone, and build trust. It's the skill behind smooth rapport and tough negotiations alike. EQ makes you not just heard — but felt.

8. Long-Term Vision – Think Beyond the Close

The goal isn't just to close the deal — it's to build a client for life. The best reps stay visible, follow up even after the sale, and earn referrals by showing real care.

9. Solution-Oriented Thinking – Find a Way Forward

Obstacles are part of the job. Instead of stalling, top sellers get creative. They reframe, reposition, or re-engage. When one door closes, they find another.

10. Adaptability – Thrive in Change

Markets shift. Tech evolves. Clients change direction. The best salespeople don't resist — they respond. They stay relevant by staying open and flexible.

Mindset isn't fluff — it's your foundation. Every sales skill sits on top of your belief system, your habits, and how you respond under pressure.

11. Extreme Ownership – Make the Deal Happen

Whether it's internal approvals, follow-ups, or product delays — the mindset of ownership changes everything. Great salespeople don't wait for someone else to clear the path. They move fast, solve problems, and take full responsibility for outcomes. In many cases, that initiative is what gets the deal signed.

Skills may open the door, but mindset decides whether you walk through it.

Pro Tip: Keeping your physical fitness a priority — no matter how busy you are — is one of the simplest ways to build a stronger mindset. Fitness fuels focus, sharpens discipline, and builds the resilience you need to handle stress, rejection, and pressure. That's not just philosophy — it's science. I'm deeply passionate about fitness, and it has always helped me manage stress, stay focused, and bounce back from rejection. Be a physically fit salesperson — you'll feel the difference.

THANK YOU –
YOU MADE IT!

If you've made it this far, let me pause and say — well done.

Most people download books. Some people skim books. You actually read one — and that puts you ahead of the pack already.

By now, you've not only picked up practical B2B sales skills...
You've also:

- Challenged your mindset
- Learned to lead better sales conversations
- Seen how deals are built (not begged for)
- And realized that closing is earned — not tricked into happening

You've invested in your growth. And trust me — that's rare.

Now What?

If you're ready to keep going, I've got a few bonus chapters waiting for you:

- A little wisdom (and warning signs) from the salespeople you'll meet in the real world

- Some laughs — because sales is way too serious without humor

- And a link to even more tools and templates online to make your daily sales grind smoother

Let's wrap this up — but remember - Selling is a skill. Mastery is a mindset. And both take consistency. Thanks again for reading — see you in the bonus zone!

BONUS CHAPTER 1: WHAT YOU CAN LEARN FROM GREAT (AND TERRIBLE) SALESPEOPLE

Not all learning comes from books. A lot of it happens on the sales floor, in meetings, during calls — and by simply watching how others sell.

Some reps will inspire you. Others... not so much. But both are valuable teachers — if you're paying attention.

What You Can Learn from Great Salespeople

Great salespeople often don't have flashy tricks. Instead, they do the basics *brilliantly*:

- They ask thoughtful questions that get the client talking.

- They know their product inside out — and more importantly, when *not* to talk about it.

- They listen more than they speak.

- They build trust without forcing it.
- They always follow up — but never in a needy or desperate way.
- They make the client feel like they're buying, not being sold.

Take notes. Ask questions. Learn what works — and why it works.

Warning Signs of Bad Sales Habits (Watch and Avoid)

Sometimes, you'll see bad sales habits that get temporarily rewarded — but don't be fooled. Here are a few red flags to watch out for:

- Fake urgency: "This offer is only valid today" (when it isn't).

- Overpromising: Saying "yes" to everything just to get the deal.

- Feature dumping: Talking non-stop about product features without asking a single question.

- Client shaming: Making the buyer feel stupid for not understanding the solution.

- Neglecting post-sale care: Disappearing after the contract is signed.

- Hiding behind jargon: Trying to sound smart instead of making things clear.

You may see some of these people hit short-term targets. But they rarely build long-term trust — or careers.

Observe. Adapt. Don't Copy Blindly.

It's easy to copy what the "top rep" does — but remember, you don't always see the full picture.

They may have an advantage you don't (years of rapport, pricing leverage, an inherited pipeline, or a brand reputation). Instead of copying behavior, copy the principles behind it.

Don't just ask: *"What do they do?"*
Ask: *"Why does that work — and
does it fit my style?"*

Your sales success will come from learning,
adapting, and developing your own authentic
style — not mimicking someone else's.

Final Thought:
Sometimes, the most valuable sales lesson comes from watching a terrible rep completely blow a deal. If you're paying attention, you'll learn more from their mistakes than your own.

Just stay humble. Stay curious. And keep learning.

BONUS CHAPTER 2:
THE B2B SALES CODE

10 Personal Rules to Sell With Integrity

Success in B2B sales isn't just about hitting targets — it's about how you get there.

These aren't tactics. They're not trends.
They're timeless principles that keep you grounded, trusted, and proud of the work you do.

If you want to build a meaningful, long-lasting career in sales — let these be your internal code.

The B2B Sales Code

1. **Never sell something you don't understand.**
   If you can't explain the solution clearly, you're not ready to sell it.

2. **Always listen more than you speak.**
   The best sales pitch is often a well-timed question.

3. **Prepare before every call — even the "quick ones."**
   Winging it is not a strategy. Every conversation deserves respect.

4. **Don't chase — qualify.**
   Not every lead is worth your time. Know when to walk.

5. **Protect your energy.**
   Burnout helps no one. Prioritize wisely and recharge often.

6. **Don't overpromise.**
   Trust is hard to build — and very easy to lose.

7. **Stay curious.**
   About the client, the industry, your craft — curiosity keeps you sharp.

8. **Give before you ask.**
   Share insights. Offer value. Build goodwill.

9. **Sell to solve.**
   If you're not helping them improve, don't ask for their money.

10. **Leave people better than you found them.**
    Even if they don't buy — let them remember your professionalism, not your pitch.

The best salespeople don't just close deals — they build reputations.

Live by a code that makes people want to work with you again... and again.

Let Us End with Some More Laugh

#1 OBJECTION HANDLING - THE MILLION DOLLAR INDUSTRY AND THE MAGIC WANDS FROM THE SALES COACHING GURUS

Objection Handling: The Billion-Dollar Industry Built on One-Liners

Let's be honest: no modern sales book would feel complete without the magical art of "objection handling," right?

Except — I left it out. On purpose. For two reasons:

1. It's too complex to cover meaningfully in one book — there are more variations than coffee orders at Starbucks.

2. More importantly…

I don't really believe in it. (There, I said it.)

Just like negotiation, **objections shouldn't be the focus — they should be the exception.**

If you're doing your job properly in discovery, demo, and budget alignment, there shouldn't be many objections left to "handle."

In fact, persistent objections often mean just one thing:
The buyer isn't ready to buy. And no magic one-liner will change that.

Still, let's have a little fun.
Here are **3 classic objections** — and how the billion-dollar coaching industry trains you to "melt them away"...
versus how things actually go down in the real world of B2B sales.

Objection A: "I'll think about it."

What it really means in B2B:

- They're not fully convinced about your solution.

- They're comparing other vendors.

- They don't feel the urgency to make a decision.

Guru-approved response:

> *"Can I ask — what specifically do you need to think about?"*
> - beware of this, you will probably be thrown out of the room if the C Level heavy weights are sitting on the other side of the table.

Real-world result of this response:
A polite smile followed by... *"We'll get back to you."* Or worse: **radio silence.**

What actually works:
Stay calm and ask:

> *"Totally fine — do you have a time frame in mind for deciding on next steps?"*
> (Notice: not *"deciding to buy"*, just *"next steps."*)

Asking for a decision makes people defensive.
Asking for a next step makes them feel in control — and you get

clarity.

If they give you a timeline, great. Follow up accordingly.

If they don't? It's probably not a priority — politely move them to the low-priority list and **focus on real prospects.**

Objection B: "We don't have the budget."

What it really means:

- Your solution is a good fit, but feels expensive.

- They're shopping around and you're not the cheapest.

- There's no urgency right now to implement this solution.

Guru trick:

> *"Can you really afford NOT to solve this problem?"*

Yeah… try that on a mid-level manager who just had their department's budget slashed.

What works better:

Be human. Be honest.

> *"I understand. Would you be comfortable sharing your investment plan for such projects so I can see what's possible — or if we should revisit this at a later stage?"*

If they give you a number — perfect. You can evaluate, reframe, adjust scope, or walk away.

If they say they're "unsure," that's usually code for *"not urgent."*

Ask for a follow-up time in a month or quarter — and move on. Respectfully.

Objection C: "I need to discuss this with my spouse!"

LOL! If someone tells you this in B2B, just close the laptop and go for a walk (or coffee).

In B2B, this objection takes a more professional disguise:

"I need to check with my manager/leadership team."

What it really means:

- You're talking to a **researcher, not a decision-maker**.

- They're gathering info — or stalling.

- You might be too early in the sales cycle.

Don't get annoyed. Don't push.
Just say:

"Absolutely. Would it help if I shared anything additional to support your internal discussion?"

Then ask:

"When would be a good time for us to reconnect after you've spoken with them?"

That's it. You can't force authority. You can only support the process and **decide where to invest your time.** Put them in your regular follow up list. Always focus on building a trusted business relationship.

Final Thought on Objection Handling

Objection handling is a good skill to have — it's just not the **main skill.**
If you're constantly battling objections, it's a sign to revisit your discovery, value message, or qualification approach.

Because when you sell the right way, objections aren't roadblocks — they're rare.

And when they *do* show up, don't try to outsmart them with a "killer script."
Just be respectful, clear, and honest — it works better than 90% of guru playbooks.

Now go close smart — and laugh when you hear, *"We'll get back to you."*
Because you already know what that means.

#2 SALES COURSES YOU SHOULD NEVER WASTE YOUR TIME ON (EVEN IF THEY'RE FREE)

You've seen them. You've probably been targeted by at least five today.

"I've built over ten 7-figure businesses... now I just want to give away my system for free."
Sponsored by: Facebook Ads
(*Translation:* It's not charity. It's a lead magnet to sell you a $20-$99 "masterclass.") - you can also imagine, Warren Buffet is running an FB paid promo titled *"I have earned 150 Billion + through investing, let's join my masterclass where I'll reveal the secret"* - Never happens!

"Finally revealing my no cold call, no cold email system — just set it and watch the sales roll in!"
Must be using Aladdin's lamp. And somehow they're handing it to strangers on Zoom.

"No calling. No emailing. Just use AI. It'll find your leads and close them for you while you sleep."
Clearly a system from the year 3050 that time-traveled back to save modern salespeople. Still waiting on delivery.

"I escaped my 9-to-5. Now I travel the world and work from anywhere using this digital business."
A business with no website, no product, no brand, and no actual explanation. Just vibes. Welcome to MLM land.

"100% passive income sales system. No product, no meetings, no selling. Just sign up and watch the cash flow in."
If this actually worked, why are they still running $15 ads trying to convince you?

"This email copy made me $1.2 million. Join the free masterclass to learn how."
What they don't mention: that email was sent to a 200,000-person list built from five years of paid ads, paid traffic, and affiliate promos.
Also… no one reads email that long anymore.

If the course title sounds like a sci-fi movie, a get-rich fantasy, or something your uncle's friend from WhatsApp is promoting — walk away. Or at least mute the tab, engage in prospecting rather.

Real sales is real work. But when done right, it brings real freedom too — just without the lamp.

END WORDS – THANK YOU, AND KEEP GOING

"It's not who I am underneath, but what I do that defines me" – Batman/The Dark Knight

If you're still reading — thank you.

You've made it through a full, honest, real-world guide to B2B solution selling. I've done my best to share not just tactics, but mindset, mistakes, and lessons learned through years of doing the work, not just talking about it.

I hope this book gave you practical tools, clarity, and a renewed belief in your own growth. But this is just a starting point.

Most importantly — **keep learning**.
Every day, every call, every prospect teaches you something. Stay curious, stay sharp, and don't let setbacks define you.

Because let's face it — **sales is tough**.
You carry the pressure of targets, deadlines, and expectations. You represent your company's revenue, reputation, and future. That's no small task.

To thrive in sales, you need more than just skills.
You need resilience. Mental endurance. And a mindset that lets you grow without burning out.

Your job is hard — but your growth is worth it.
Keep evolving. Keep giving your best. And remember: the most fulfilled salespeople aren't just closers — they're problem-solvers, learners, and trusted advisors.

SHAH IMRUL

See you on the journey.

POST CREDIT SCENE

Just when you thought the movie was over...

So — you've found the perfect prospect.
You nailed the discovery call.
Your demo got applause.
The budget? A match made in sales heaven.
The proposal? Sent and approved.
And now — a glorious **Purchase Order** lands in your inbox. Time to pop the champagne? **Not yet.**
Ask yourself one question:

Has the payment hit your company's bank account?

If not, keep the cork in the bottle.

In B2B sales, **the deal isn't done until the money moves.**
Delays happen. Paperwork stalls. Priorities shift. Budgets freeze. Until the payment is confirmed, stay sharp, stay present, and keep your radar active.

Celebrate too early, and you might be toasting a ghost deal.

Stay mindful — and good luck out there!